WALKING AN ANCIENT PATH

WALKING AN ANCIENT PATH

Exploring four key New Testament Texts about Jesus

Alex Jacob

The Church's Ministry among Jewish People (CMJ)

Glory to Glory Publications

First published in Great Britain by
Glory to Glory Publications
an imprint of
Buy Research Ltd.
PO Box 212 SAFFRON WALDEN CB10 2UU

ISBN 978-0-9926674-4-3

Printed in Great Britain by
Imprint Digital, Exeter
and worldwide by CreateSpace

Contents

	Dedication	7
	Acknowledgements	9
	Introduction	11
1.	John 1:1–18	15
2.	Philippians 2:6–11	29
3.	Colossians 1:15–20	39
4.	Hebrews 1:1–4	45
5.	Exploring Christian mission and our understanding of God	55
	(a) Taking the first steps – back to the beginning	
	(b) Talking along the way – joining in with a missional conversation	
	(c) Thinking more thoughts – a little more theology for the walk ahead	
	Some resources for reflection	65
	Bibliography	69

DEDICATION

In loving memory of Bishop John B Taylor
6th May 1926 – 1st June 2016
Patron of CMJ/Bishop of St Albans

"The Lord will be king over the whole earth. On that day there will be one Lord and his name the only name."
(Zechariah 14:9)

Acknowledgements

As I began this new book project (my ninth major writing project) while working with The Church's Ministry among Jewish People (CMJ), I was very much aware of how one is helped to think and study by the example and encouragement of colleagues. Within the CMJ mission network there are many inspiring people doing important pioneering ministry: Thank you for the example you have given and for the support you offer.

I would like to thank especially my wife Mandy and our three grown-up children, Luke, Emily and Ben: Your kindness, care and support are so encouraging to me. Also once again I want to acknowledge the kind guidance and practical help of Rev Dr David Moore, members and friends from Linton United Reformed Church, Peter Sammons and the Glory to Glory publishing team.

Introduction

At the very heart of Christian faith and life is the person and work of Jesus (Yeshua). The study of the person and work of Jesus is known within theological circles as Christology. Christology is fundamental to Christian Theology.

Theology should not be viewed as a dry, dull or remote academic pursuit, but rather it should be experienced and enjoyed as an essential part of Christian discipleship, for theology is about (or should be!) *faith seeking understanding*. In addition to that definition I am also drawn to the definition offered by Mark Kinzer, who states: *Theology is not a 'detached science' but a 'personal struggle' to conform our minds to what G-d has revealed and continues to reveal about Himself, His will, His works and His relationship to us, and what it means for us and our community in our present historical and social juncture.*[1]

Christology connects and overlaps with many other areas of theological study such as Theodicy (the study of the doctrine of God in a theistic tradition),[2] Pneumatology (the study of the person and work of the Holy Spirit), Ecclesiology (the study of the doctrine of the Church) and Soteriology (the study of atonement, salvation and redemption).

As one opens the New Testament the reality of *who Jesus is* and *what He does* is central to the unfolding narrative and teaching. Clearly the view one holds (and one's consequent action) with regard to the person and work of Jesus shapes who we are (and who we will be) and the faith community we belong to and identify with. What view we hold and the understanding we share about Jesus is the key demarcation point in God's dealing with His creation. This has always been the case, from the earliest ministry period of Jesus (see for example John 7:43) right up until the present time.

This demarcation point is true and valid in all mission encounters, but arguably it has a particularly prominence in Jewish-Christian relations and within Christian and Islamic encounters, as in these situations one explores the understanding of God in a monotheistic faith context. In regard to Jewish-Christian Relations, the Messianic Jewish theologian Jacob Jocz reflected deeply upon this monotheistic faith context and wrote: *At the centre of the controversy between the Church and the Synagogue stands the Christological question. This is not a question of whether Jesus is the Messiah, but whether the Christian understanding of the Messiah is admissible in view of the Jewish concept of God. Here lies the dividing line between Judaism and Christianity. On this point neither can afford to compromise.*[3]

In my recent thinking and reflection on Jesus, and my beginning to walk along the ancient path of Christological study, I have been helped and encouraged by four things.

Firstly, I am acutely aware that in any theological study one enters into areas of mystery. Soon one is taken beyond one's own 'comfort zone' of understanding as the bigger picture of God's revelation stretches one beyond one's own insights and beyond the limitations of one's own words. This is certainly true as one glimpses into the big picture of Jesus – His grace, beauty, loving kindness, truth and power.

For myself, I am reminded, in walking along this path of Christological study and reflection, that the path is one which began many miles before I came upon its traces, and will end miles after I will need to stop – lost in wonder and praise. Therefore I am encouraged that whatever I share is only a small part of the much greater journey. I hope we will all enjoy this part of the walk!

Secondly, I have attended a lecture series[4] on Christology presented by Rowan Williams. The series was called 'Christ and the logic of Creation'. Through these lectures a concise historical and theological survey of Christological developments was given. Within this survey one glimpses the ideas about Jesus which have arisen through travelling along a path illuminated by revelation, reflection and missionary apologetics. Rowan Williams helped those of us on the course to engage with key figures who have walked along this path before us and in many cases have set up marker posts or signposts – figures such as Paul, John of Damascus, Augustine, Aquinas , Calvin, Barth, Forsyth, Bonhoeffer and Moltmann (to name but a few).

Thirdly, I have read and reflected widely around issues of Christology and the Trinity, primarily in a Christian-Jewish context. I have found a number of books especially helpful, for example: *The Divine Name(s) and the Holy Trinity* by R Kendall Soulen; *The Trinity – An Essential for Faith in Our Time,* edited by Andrew Stirling; *The Divinity of the Messiah* by Joseph Frey; *The Jewish Trinity* by Yoel Natan, and *The One, The Three and The Many* by Colin Gunton. For full details of these books, please turn to the bibliography.

Fourthly, I have read again, and discussed with colleagues and friends, the key Christological texts of the New Testament. In discussing and exploring these texts, I understand that it is in the New Testament where Christological and Trinitarian thought and language begin formally (yet there is nothing in the absolute monotheism of the Old Testament that contradicts this formal beginning). Clearly, for me, the teachings in the Bible are progressive as the covenantal faithfulness of God is revealed and applied throughout salvation history. Most Biblical commentators agree that there are four such Christological texts, namely: John 1:1–18, Philippians 2:6–11,

Colossians 1:15–20 and Hebrews 1:1–4. It is to these four texts which we will now turn in this brief study.

Notes

[1] Mark Kinzer, *The Shape of Messianic Jewish Theology:* Session 1: What is Messianic Jewish Theology (course material MJ 518, MJTI, Fuller School of Theology, 2004).

[2] Within this area of study there is often an attempt to explain and vindicate God's nature and activity.

[3] Jacob Jocz, *The Invisibility of God and the Incarnation* in *The Messiahship of Jesus,* edited by Arthur Kac (Baker Books, 1986).

[4] These open public lectures were hosted by Cambridge University Divinity School during the spring term, 2016.

Exploring the first key Christological text
John 1:1-18

The four key Christological texts all share much insight. There is a rich unity, yet each text has its own unique emphasis and specific focus. It is fascinating to begin to compare and contrast these texts. As is the case for all four, I will begin by setting out the text in full, using two Biblical translations, namely the New International Version (NIV) and the Messianic Jewish Family Bible (MJFB). In most cases in this book, I will quote from the NIV. I have selected these two translations as I am familiar with them both and have found them to be very helpful through various study projects. However, I would encourage anyone reading this study book to seek out other translations and commentaries (please turn to the bibliography for details). We begin with John 1:1–18.

In the beginning was the Word, and the Word was with God, and the Word was God. He was with God in the beginning. Through him all things were made; without him nothing was made that has been made. In him was life, and that life was the light of men. The light shines in the darkness, but the darkness has not understood it. There came a man who was sent from God; his name was John. He came as a witness to testify concerning the light, so that through him all men might believe. He himself was not the light; he came only as a witness to the light. The true light that gives light to every man was coming into the world.

He was in the world, and though the world was made through him, the world did not recognise him. He came to that which was his own, but his own did not receive

him. Yet to all who received him, to those who believed in his name, he gave the right to become children of God – children born not of natural descent, nor of human decision or a husband's will, but born of God.

The Word became flesh and made his dwelling among us. We have seen his glory, the glory of the One and Only, who came from the Father, full of grace and truth.

John testifies concerning him. He cries out, saying, "This was he of whom I said, 'He who comes after me has surpassed me because he was before me.'" From the fullness of his grace we have all received one blessing after another. For the law was given through Moses; grace and truth came through Jesus Christ. No one has ever seen God, but God the One and Only, who is at the Father's side, has made him known.

John 1:1–18 (NIV)

In the beginning was the Word. The Word was with God, and the Word was God. He was with God in the beginning. All things were made through Him, and apart from Him nothing was made that has come into being. In Him was life, and the life was the light of men. The light shines in the darkness, and the darkness has not overpowered it.

There came a man sent from God, whose name was John. He came as a witness to testify about the light, so that through him everyone might believe. He was not the light, but he came to bear witness concerning the light. The true light, coming into the world, gives light to every man.

He was in the world, and the world was made through Him; but the world did not know Him. He came to His own, but His own did not receive Him. But whoever did receive Him, those trusting in His name, to these He gave the right to become children of God. They were born not of a bloodline, nor of human desire, nor of man's will,

but of God. And the Word became flesh and tabernacled among us. We looked upon His glory, the glory of the one and only from the Father, full of grace and truth.

John testifies about Him. He cried out, saying, "This is He of whom I said, 'The One who comes after me is above me, because He existed before me.'" Out of His fullness, we have all received grace on top of grace. Torah was given through Moses; grace and truth came through Yeshua the Messiah. No one has ever seen God; but the one and only God, in the Father's embrace, has made Him known.

John 1:1–18 (MJFB)

Setting the Scene for John's Gospel

Every commentator on a Biblical text needs to explore and to try and offer some answers to at least four basic questions – these are sometimes referred to as the four introductory 'W's – namely, 'Who wrote it?', 'When was it written?', 'Where was it written?' and 'Why was it written?' In some cases apparently clear answers for all four questions are presented by each commentator (although they do not always agree with each other!) while in other cases (such as the authorship of Hebrews) there seems to be little certainty to any of the 'answers' offered.

With respect to the four introductory questions regarding John's Gospel, I would encourage you to read widely around various commentaries, but let me try to set the scene by offering you my four 'answers'.

Who wrote John's Gospel? I would argue it was John the apostle whom Jesus loved (John 13:23, 19:26, 20:2). This John was a cousin of Jesus and the brother of James, who was also a disciple of Jesus. John was a prominent disciple and part of an 'inner circle' which included Peter and James. John became a well-known leader in the early Church community, but is not mentioned by name in the text – this would seem understandable if John was the author, but it is less easy to explain if he was not. I think this John is also the author of the three New Testament letters of John and the book of Revelation.

As to dating, I would suggest it should be between the mid 50s and no later than the late 60s.

With regard to the place of writing, the traditional view, based in part on the testimony of Irenaeus (AD 130–200) which I find convincing, is that John wrote while he was living in Ephesus.

The final 'W', exploring the 'why' question, deals with the purpose and character of the writing and is a much wider question than the previous three. In simple terms, this Gospel is written, as stated in 20:31, that, *you may believe that Jesus is the Christ, the Son of God, and that by believing you may have life in his name*. However, this answer is probably no different from the core purpose of any of the New Testament writings. It seems we need to walk a little further.

John has a dual role in writing: clearly he hopes that his writing will help non-believers and those searching to find faith and to come to believe in Jesus. The term *to believe* or *believing* occurs frequently in the text (98 times) and this is far more than in Matthew, Mark and Luke combined. It should be noted that the words of Jesus are often presented in keeping with the style of an evangelist, and a clear and persistent 'evangelistic thread' runs through the selection of material John uses. In this regard, however, it should be noted that Jesus does not directly bring people to Himself, but rather His disciples or those who have encountered Him (such as the Samaritan woman in John 4) bring would-be disciples to Him, and Jesus then affirms and welcomes them. We see this pattern in the case of Andrew helping Philip, and then Philip helping Nathanael to meet with and then to follow Jesus (John 1:40–45).

In addition to this clear evangelistic intent, it should also be noted that there is at least one other clear purpose within John's Gospel – namely to equip believers to *keep on believing* (this makes better sense of the Greek 'present continuous' tense of 20:31), and to maintain and grow in their trust in, obedience to, and love for, Jesus. Some of these believers may have been faced with heretical teaching and cultural pressures, whether from the non-Messianic rabbinical Jewish world or the wider Greek/Roman world.

John may well have had such false teaching and cultural pressures in his mind and sought to address some of them through his presentation of Jesus and the selection of his material, in order to enable his readers to grasp the truth and hold on to the truth and to live out the truth – for Jesus Himself is the truth!

Turning to the text

It is clear from the opening verses of John's Gospel that it is different from the other three ('synoptic') Gospels. Matthew and Luke begin with placing the birth of Jesus into a specific historical context (the birth stories) and both have unique insights. Matthew, for example, uniquely records the visit of the Magi and the flight of the holy family into Egypt. For his part, by contrast, Luke tells of Mary's visit to Elizabeth, the shepherds and the angels, and concludes the birth narrative with the presentation of Jesus in the Temple. Mark has no birth narrative but simply and directly begins with a declaration of who Jesus is (Mark 1:1), and then turns to the public ministry of John the Baptist (linking back to Isaiah's prophecy), and concludes the opening segment with a focus on the promise that the one more powerful than John will come with a baptism of the Holy Spirit. John, however, begins with a prologue (1:1–18) which proclaims the wider theological context behind the birth stories.

It is worth noting that all four Gospels give a significant role to the preparatory ministry of John the Baptist. He is often spoken of as the *forerunner* (*prodromos* in Greek) and this word conveys very strong relational terms – in the sense that, while one is thinking about the 'forerunner' one automatically begins to think of the one who will follow. In the Gospel context, to think of John the Baptist is to think of Jesus.

As one reads this prologue to the Gospel it becomes clear that John has gained a very specific revelation about the person of Jesus. Here we encounter key words and terms, such as: *in the beginning*, *the Word*, *light*, *life*, *glory*, *fullness*, *Word became flesh, dwelling among us* and *at the Father's side*. From where and from whom did such insights come? Did John receive a direct revelation through a vision or dream, or was it via an angel, as was the case with the book of Revelation? (See Revelation 1:1). Or was it based in part on John's own prayerful reflections on the times he followed and shared with Jesus during His public ministry? Or maybe (as I have suggested in my book *Prepare the Way!*),[1] Mary the mother of Jesus might well have been a key source.

Why suggest Mary? Firstly, she had a deep knowledge of Scripture. The prayer of praise she sings (Luke 1:46–55) is full of Scriptural references and draws in many ways from Hannah's song[2] (see 1 Samuel 2), and she quotes directly from Psalm 34:2 and Psalm 35:9. Soon after this, she travels with Joseph to the Temple and fulfils the requirements of the Torah (Luke 2:22–24).

Secondly, we also know that Mary treasured Jesus. She treasured and pondered all the things said about Jesus and all the events surrounding His birth and subsequent upbringing and ministry. Also we are told (only in John's Gospel) that Mary was at the crucifixion of Jesus (John 19:25) and that she witnessed His agonising death. Finally, Luke records in Acts 1:14 that Mary was part of the emerging Church community which proclaimed His resurrection, ascension and Lordship.

It is impossible to know how this embryonic early Church community was blessed and encouraged by Mary's presence and her insights, but we know that Mary was cared for by John in Ephesus. It is my suggestion that John and Mary shared many conversations together. Based in part on these treasured conversations, John chooses to begin his Gospel, not with a simple re-telling of the birth events (as told in part by Matthew and Luke), but rather by bringing out the true meaning, majesty and significance of the birth of Jesus – namely: *In the beginning was the Word and the Word was with God, and the Word was God ... The Word became flesh and made his dwelling among us. We have seen his glory.* Maybe the 'we' of John 1:14 here refers not only to the wider context (embracing all Christ's followers), but specifically to John, who was an eyewitness to much of the public ministry of Jesus, and to Mary, who was an eyewitness to his private birth and upbringing.

Turning to the text, the structure is particularly well crafted, with a poetic style. The careful crafting of the text is intriguing, and there are many other examples of such careful crafting throughout the Gospel. Especially intriguing is the threefold use of lists of seven. There are seven witnesses who all have a personal testimony to the truth about the person and/or ministry of Jesus. The seven are: John the Baptist, who is introduced in the prologue, Nathanael, Peter, Martha, Thomas, John (the disciple Jesus loved) and Jesus Himself.

Then we have seven miracles (perhaps better described as divine signs) in John's Gospel, which point to the power and purpose of the ministry of Jesus. These signs, in order of the text, are: turning water into wine at Cana; healing of the royal official's son at Capernaum; healing of the long-term ill man at the Pool of Bethesda in Jerusalem; feeding the 5,000 in Galilee; walking on the water on the Lake of Galilee; healing the man blind from birth near the Temple courts in Jerusalem, and then the raising from the dead of Lazarus at Bethany.

Finally, we have the seven main 'I AM' sayings which most commentators perceive as 'self-testimonies' to the ministry and mission of Jesus. These seven sayings are: *I am the bread of life* (6:35); *I am the light of the world* (8:12 and in 9:5); *I am the gate* (10:7); *I am the good shepherd* (10:11, and in 10:14); *I am the resurrection and the life* (11:25); *I am the way, the truth and the life* (14:6); and, finally, *I am the true vine* (15:1, and *I am the vine* in 15:5). These sayings which linked Jesus to God by making reference to the divine name of YHWH (Exodus 3:13–16) hold the teaching material of the Gospel in a coherent framework, for the Gospel begins with *the Word was God* (1:1), and draws to an end with the faith statement of Thomas: *My Lord and my God!* (20:28).

Some commentators, such as Jerome Neyrey, have made out a case that the structure from verses 12–18 is providing the reader with a chiastic framework. A 'chiasm' is a deliberate arrangement of a text in an 'X' shape, based on the Greek letter *chi*, which is so shaped. The text is arranged in a way which gives special places to parallel words at the top and bottom of the text (A to A). This is then added to by other parallels (B to B, C to C, etc.). This structure in turn draws attention to a central passage which conveys the core message.

Most commentators who promote this chiastic framework and who also believe it is not simply ornamental, but rather deliberately shapes the meaning, tend to see seven pairs of parallels in this text, which trace the movement of the Word from being 'in God' to the descent into 'flesh'. The central message is the precise moment in time when the testimony of John the Baptist gives witness to the light as the light enters this world.

In regard to time, it is worth noting that John precedes Jesus in linear (chronological) time (who *comes after me*) yet his witness emphasises the eternal priority of Jesus (*he was before me*). This chiastic framework may be a valuable insight, but the value and impact of the text does not depend on the validity of this structure.

Verses 1–5

The text begins at the beginning! The phrase *in the beginning* would lead all who are well versed in the Scriptures to think back to Genesis 1:1. 'In the beginning' points to a 'time' before creation, and in this the reader or hearer is given a glimpse into eternity from a heavenly 'time' perspective.

Linked to this beginning is the Word (*logos* in Greek). The concept of the Word may be understood in two main ways. For the Jewish reader, the concept would point primarily to God or a supernatural being. The text declares that the Word relates to God and shares all the power and attributes of God. In this sense John goes further than any concept found in the wisdom texts of the Old Testament (*Tanakh*) by declaring *the Word was God*. By doing this, John roots the divinity of Jesus back beyond the resurrection (Acts 2:26 and Romans 1:4), back beyond His transfiguration (Mark 9:7), back beyond His baptism (Mark 1:11), back even beyond His birth (Matthew 1:20–23; Luke 1:35; 2:10–14). In doing this, John shows the pre-existence of the Word and His relationship to God. For John, if God created *in the beginning* then the uncreated Son was also present and active *in the beginning*.

The Word is spoken and creation *ex nihilo* (out of nothing) happens. This understanding of Creation is the supreme poetic declaration of the power of the Creator. This understanding is rooted in the Genesis text and in Psalm 33:6–9, Psalm 147:18 and Isaiah 55:11. For the Greek, however, the term 'Word' would stir up thoughts about reason and the rational processes and principles which govern all things. John does not define his use of the term *Word* at this stage, but maybe he is deliberately using a term which would have a helpful meaning to intrigue (and therefore draw in) both Jewish and Greek thinkers.

John then describes the work of the Word in creation. Here we hear echoes of Colossians 1:15–20 and Hebrews 1:1–4, texts we will look at later, but in John the vast scale of this creative act is shown (note the word *all* within the prologue, in vv. 3, 7, 12 and 15), and by reflecting upon this creative act, two key themes of John's Gospel are introduced, namely *life* and *light*.

Verses 6–13

The phrase *there came a man* (referring to John the Baptist) brings the divine declaration of verses 1–5 into an earthly focus. In one sense John brings us down to earth with an almighty bump! There is something almost scandalous as one hears of the immortal becoming mortal and the holy becoming part of a community of humanity. Here the great acts of creation and salvation are to be worked out through humanity, through history, through flesh and blood. John the Baptist becomes the key prophetic witness to the incarnation of Jesus, just as a little later the apostles will become the prime witnesses to the resurrection and ascension of Jesus.

John the apostle clearly honours John the Baptist as a prophet, yet prevents us from developing too high a view of the Baptist's ministry by declaring that John the Baptist was not the light of the world, but rather only pointed to the light. (A false high view may well be seen from the attitude of John the Baptist's disciples in Acts 19:1ff., where it appears that a sect was growing which venerated John the Baptist and ignored – or knew very little about – Jesus and the gospel message. The events recorded in Acts 19 take place in Ephesus, the city in which John the apostle was living, so maybe John the apostle was well aware of this sect growing up around the honouring of the memory and teaching of John the Baptist).

The light comes into the world. This is the true light (perhaps in contrast to the many false lights and false prophetic claims which demand a hearing), but while this light has worldwide significance, the light does not find worldwide acceptance. Yet John the apostle declares that there were those who received the light and believed in His name – to these He gave the right (authority) to become children of God. For John the term 'to believe in his name' means to believe in everything Jesus is and does. The fuller implications of this spiritual reality – this being born of God – are taught by John when he tells of the meeting between Jesus and Nicodemus (John 3).

Verses 14-18

The phrase *The Word became flesh* continues to help unfold how the great event of salvation is being worked out through humanity, through history, through flesh and blood. The focus on the Word becoming flesh conveys a compelling sense of transition. The Word existed before becoming a human being. In the beginning was the Word (1:1). Yet the eternal Word came and dwelt among humanity, becoming fully human.

This Greek word for *dwelling* has links with the word tent or tabernacle and is meant to remind us of the tabernacle in the Exodus events (Exodus 40:34–38) and to apply this to the Incarnation. Maybe there are other links as well, for example to the prophetic ministry of Samuel at Shiloh and the ongoing events surrounding the Ark of the Covenant. I think the MJFB translation is very helpful here in retaining the term *tabernacled among us*. My paraphrase of this would be that *Jesus came and pitched his tent right in the centre of our camp*. This emphasis on the Tent of Meeting is helpful for two main reasons. Firstly, it links the person and work of

Jesus in with the promises and purposes of the Tabernacle and later the Temple. The Tabernacle and the Temple provide a theological framework within the covenantal purposes of God. This is clearly so in the epistle to the Hebrews, but also in the Gospels, for we see so much of the ministry of Jesus linked to the Temple. For example, Luke's Gospel begins and ends in the Temple, while the cleansing of the Temple features prominently in all four Gospels.[3]

The relationship of Jesus with the Temple is an intriguing one. As a Jewish child brought up within a faithful Jewish family, He had a great connection with the Temple, its ministry and traditions. He was consecrated in the Temple, he went there as a child, and maybe there in the Temple the child Jesus had His first awareness of His special relationship with the Father and with His own calling. Did the words Jesus spoke, *Didn't you know I had to be in my Father's house*? (Luke 2:50) seem to suggest such an awakening of core identity, or at least a deepening of an existing understanding? Later, Jesus taught within the Temple courts and visited the Temple frequently during the pilgrim festivals of Passover, Pentecost and Tabernacles. Yet Jesus also refined and challenged many of the prevailing understandings and practices of the Temple.

Jesus taught that He Himself is the true Temple. It was probably this claim alongside His claim of divinity which led to his arrest based on charges for blasphemy and related subversive political acts and aims. This sense of being the true Temple is then widened by Paul, who offers perhaps the clearest definition of what a Christian is, namely *the temple of the Holy Spirit* (2 Corinthians 6:16). In this affirmation, Christian theologians declare that pneumatology is immanent Christology. Or, in more simple terms, the Holy Spirit is the Spirit of the now ascended Jesus. The gift of the Holy Spirit cannot simply be seen as a gift from God but is a gift of God. The Holy Spirit does not make up for the absence of Jesus, but rather brings His presence into the life of each Christian and into the community life of the Church. This great Christological and Trinitarian truth can be traced back to John's declaration that *the Word became flesh and made his dwelling among us*.

Secondly, the emphasis on 'tabernacled among us' makes a connection with the pilgrim festival of Tabernacles, which is celebrated each autumn. As stated above, there is a link between the ministry of Jesus in the Temple and the times of the three pilgrim festivals. However, there may be an even greater link if we see how the timing of the festivals finds a direct fulfilment in the ministry of Jesus. This fulfilment is clear in the case of Passover, with the link to the Last Supper, which is expressed in all three of the synoptic gospels (see Luke 22:8, Mark 14:12 and Matthew 26:17). Also strongly connected with the Passover is the understanding of Jesus being presented as the sacrificial Passover lamb (John 1:29). This understanding links back to Isaiah 53:7, Jeremiah 11:19 and Genesis 22:8 and is taken forward in the teaching of Paul in 1 Corinthians 5:7 and Peter in 1 Peter 1:2. In Pentecost we see the link between the giving of the Torah and the death of three thousand (Exodus 32:18), and the giving of the Holy Spirit in fullness and the baptism of three thousand (Acts 2:41). However, for most commentators there is no such link evident with the final festival, the festival of Tabernacles.

Maybe the real link which so many commentators have missed is that Jesus was born in Bethlehem during the festival of Tabernacles. Jesus tabernacled with us at Tabernacles! Some others suggest that the link with festival of Tabernacles and the birth of Jesus is tenuous, yet see a future link, namely that Jesus will return in glory at the festival of Tabernacles. My own view is that both propositions are probably true – namely that the birth of Jesus and His return both coincide with the festival of Tabernacles.

Concluding this section, we see that the tabernacle is Jesus, the eternal Word made flesh. This Jesus is the place of meeting, a place where God's presence and glory is experienced, just as it was in the tabernacle of old (see Exodus 26, 33, 40), yet now fully in the person of Jesus. God makes Himself known, and in Jesus people will see God's glory and know His presence and receive His grace (v. 14) and truth (v. 14). This awesome truth is the very essence of what John the Baptist declares and how John concludes his prologue (v. 18).

John the evangelist will continue to build on the Christology of the prologue, for example in John 8:48–59, John 10 and John 14. In this sense, I see this prologue of John's Gospel, with its movement from the eternal Word to the Son of God, both as an essential introduction to the Gospel and also as offering a conclusion to the outworking of the Gospel.

Notes

[1] Jacob Alex, *Prepare the Way!* Glory to Glory Publications, 2014.

[2] Most commentators explain the Magnificat by making this direct link to Hannah's song, but it is important also to be open to the possibility that Mary is prophesying directly under the influence of the Holy Spirit and is not consciously aware at this point of Hannah's song in the Biblical text.

[3] The timing of the cleansing of the Temple is set early in the ministry of Jesus by John (John 2:12–25) and during the final week leading up to the crucifixion by Matthew, Mark and Luke. Some commentators suggest the cleansing may have taken place on two separate occasions, namely at the beginning and towards the end of His public ministry. I explore this chronological question more fully in my book *The Case for Enlargement Theology*, p. 56.

Exploring the second key Christological text
Philippians 2:6-11

Who, being in very nature God, did not consider equality with God something to be grasped, but made himself nothing, taking the very nature of a servant, being made in human likeness. And being found in appearance as a man, he humbled himself and became obedient to death – even death on a cross! Therefore God exalted him to the highest place and gave him the name that is above every name, that at the name of Jesus every knee should bow, in heaven and on earth and under the earth, and every tongue confess that Jesus Christ is Lord, to the glory of God the Father.

Philippians 2:6–11 (NIV)

Who, though existing in the form of God, did not consider being equal to God a thing to be grasped. But He emptied Himself—taking on the form of a slave, becoming the likeness of men and being found in appearance as a man. He humbled Himself—becoming obedient to the point of death, even death on a cross. For this reason God highly exalted Him and gave Him the name, that is above every name, that at the name of Yeshua every knee should bow, in heaven and on the earth and under the earth, and every tongue profess that Yeshua the Messiah is Lord—to the glory of God the Father.

Philippians 2:6-11 (MJFB)

Setting the Scene for Philippians

In terms of the four key basic questions, the four introductory 'W's in relation to the letter to the Philippians, let me try and set the scene by offering the following four 'answers'.

Who wrote this letter? The answer is Paul the apostle. Paul is a Jew, who was born in Tarsus and possessed Roman citizenship. He grew up as a Pharisee and was a rabbinical student under Gamaliel in Jerusalem. He was strongly opposed to the new movement which had sprung up, which claimed that Jesus of Nazareth was the Messiah of Israel and Lord of all. His zeal led him to try to crush what to him was a dangerous heretical sect, yet his life and understanding was transformed when he met the risen Lord Jesus while he was travelling to Damascus. His journey had the purpose of arresting any disciple of Jesus he found in Damascus and then bringing them to trial in Jerusalem under the auspices of the High Priest (see Acts 9, 22 and 26 for more details). Following his transformation, Paul became the key missionary apostle and theologian, especially within the context of spreading the gospel westwards from Jerusalem and into many mainly Gentile settings. Paul wrote thirteen letters which are recorded in the New Testament, of which Philippians is one.

While Paul's missionary endeavours rightly mark him out as the *apostle to the Gentiles*, it is also important (I suggest) to understand that Paul maintains throughout his life an essential dual role. This role is essential to maintaining theological truth and in terms of mission strategy. An appreciation of this dual role is also vital in exploring many areas of Jewish-Christian relations today, and especially in appreciating Messianic Jewish life and thought. This dual role is based on his calling to the Gentile world, and also (which is sometimes overlooked) his calling as a prophet to Israel. Paul's theological critique of rabbinical Judaism is a critique from within the community of Israel. Throughout his life and teaching, Paul remains a faithful Jew, steeped in Torah and Scripture. He demonstrates again and again his solidarity with his Jewish people and a commitment to Israel's election within the purposes of God. This is fundamental to Paul's key teaching about Israel and the Church in Romans 9–11 and in regard to mission priorities as indicated in Romans 1:16.

Paul's authorship of this letter is also affirmed by the early Church, and the text contains many references and personal touches which all support the genuineness of Pauline authorship. The only real debate about the authorship of the letter is the suggestion made by some that it is in fact a collection of at least three letters joined together (perhaps somewhat clumsily) and presented as one single letter. A range of possible structures has been suggested in an attempt to bring some 'coherence' to the text(s). However, I do not see that this 'three letter' theory brings any interpretive insight to the text and, for me, any lack of coherence (especially Paul's apparent difficulty in concluding the letter; see how many times he writes 'finally') is not evidence of separate letters, but rather shows a spontaneous natural feel which reflects something of Paul's pastoral thinking as he dictated this somewhat personal letter.

As to dating and place of writing, a number of suggestions have been made. The earliest indicates the place of writing as Ephesus in AD 54; others make a case for Caesarea at some point from AD 57–59. I think there is some credibility in suggesting the earlier of the two dates, as the style and content (especially chapter 3) of Philippians is similar to one of Paul's earliest letters, namely Galatians, which should probably be dated around AD 48. However, on balance it is most likely that Paul is writing during the period of his house arrest in Rome, in or around AD 60–61 (he is not in prison as he was when he later wrote his second letter to Timothy), as recorded in Acts 28:14–31.

The final basic question is once again the 'Why' question. Perhaps the simplest answer is that it is primarily a 'thank-you' letter for the active support the Church at Philippi had given to Paul's ministry, and the specific gift he received to help him during his period of house arrest (Philippians 1:5 and 4:10–19). Yet Paul adds to this by sharing news of his own situation and by giving to the Church encouragement[1] and warnings, as well as commending Epaphroditus and Timothy to the Church. In this context this letter is somewhat unusual among Paul's various epistles as it does not appear to focus on specific problems or theological questions, but rather Paul is writing as a friend, which gives a unique glimpse into the depth of Paul's relationships which existed and thrived within the Church community at Philippi.

Turning to the text

In these six verses we glimpse something of the awesome mystery of Christology. Key words and phrases such as *being in the very nature God, being made in human likeness, became obedient to death*, and the key early Christian confession of faith, *Jesus Christ is Lord*, grip our attention and stir our hearts. The Greek words used here are somewhat unusual and this has led to the view that Paul is quoting from an Aramaic or Hebrew liturgical text or hymn. In various commentaries the 'hymn' is often divided up into two stanzas – stanza one in verses 6–8, and stanza two, verses 9–11.

This text or hymn may well have been widely used in Christian worship, especially while celebrating communion or baptism. Certainly the emphasis on descent (vv. 6–8) and then followed by a raising up (vv. 9–11) would fit in well with the act of a baptismal candidate entering the waters of baptism and choosing to personally identify with the death and burial of Jesus, and then rising up out of the water, thus identifying with His glorious resurrection. This liturgical understanding is well presented by many, but it should be noted that there is no external evidence for such an interpretation. Moreover, we know that Paul sometimes writes in poetic form when expressing a deep truth, so these verses may well be Paul's own poem or own hymn of praise, rather than a widely known piece of writing or shared liturgy.

For others, the text is primarily a theological creed. Clearly there is much here of theological importance, which is why we are exploring this text as one of the four key New Testament Christological texts. The verses clearly convey deep insight into the intimate relationship between Jesus and God the Father, yet no precise or formal definitions are given, as one would expect from a credal statement. On balance, I would see these words not as a liturgical song or a credal affirmation, but more in terms of a pastoral plea to inspire Christian living (see the context of the verse which precedes this text) in a way which honours and reflects the amazing choices Jesus made and the attitude He showed throughout His ministry.

Verses 6–8

The text begins with the affirmation that Jesus is God, sharing the divine nature and having all the attributes that are essential to the being and character of God. This affirmation is in keeping with other statements by Paul, such as those in Romans 9:5,[2] Romans 10:13, Titus 2:13 and the text we will explore in the next chapter, Colossians 1:15–20. Also, this verse connects back to the prologue in John, and especially John 1:1. Yet this statement is immediately followed by a somewhat perplexing phrase: *did not consider equality with God something to be grasped*. Some commentators seek to gain interpretive momentum here by finding an allusion to Adam and/or Satan. Clearly, in Scripture, both Adam and Satan sought in different ways to grasp 'equality' with God, but neither had the very nature of God as Jesus has, so the comparison is far from precise. I understand that both the phrase *equality with God* and the phrase *very nature God* are equivalent phrases and therefore the flow of the text is that the divine nature Jesus has, and the equality with God He shares, are not something which prevented Him from entering into this world as a servant and as a man.

Clearly there is an 'emptying' (*kenosis* in Greek) of the powers and privileges of divine nature in the Incarnation and especially in the death of Jesus. It is in this emptying that the divine is fully revealed and made accessible in and through the self-emptying of the crucified Jesus. In the Incarnation the eternal becomes rooted (and restricted) in time, the omnipresent becomes defined (and restricted) by place. Or to put it simply: Jesus of Nazareth could only be at one place at any one time. Also, some specific facts were unknown to Him. For example, Jesus did not know the date of His return in glory, nor who had touched him (Luke 8:43). Also, on two occasions the Gospel texts tell us that Jesus was surprised or amazed, once by the high level of faith and once by the very opposite of such faith, namely hostile unbelief (Luke 7:9 and Mark 6:6).

In His earthly life He experienced birth, growth pains, puberty, loneliness, tiredness, temptation, rejection, hunger, humiliation, and even death. This is part of the emptying, yet He did not empty himself of divinity. We must allow Scripture to help interpret Scripture, for in Colossians 1:16 we are told that all the fullness of God dwelt in Jesus of Nazareth. Also as part of this 'emptying', Jesus ministered and did mighty acts and miracles, not out of His status as God but out of His obedience to His heavenly Father and through trusting the empowering of the Holy Spirit. This emptying does not mean that Jesus in His humanity was not fully God or not fully human, but Jesus was (and is, and always will be) fully God and fully man. The key point here is that self-emptying in Jesus is never absolute. Even in (maybe especially in) His suffering and death, He remained Saviour and Lord.

Verses 9–11

From the point of emptying, of being nothing, of death, even death on a cross, God exalts Jesus. It is helpful to note that the emphasis from verses 9–11 is not upon the faithful or heroic actions of Jesus but on God's action in exalting Him. God raises Him to the highest place and gives Him the highest name. The eternal God the Son is now glorified as the exalted Son of God incarnate.

This name (or title) given for this exaltation and glorification is the name *Lord* (v. 11). The Greek word here is *kurios* and can have a range of possible meanings. It can refer to the personal name of God – tetragrammaton, YHWH – to *Lord* in the sense of a universal ruler or simply *lord* as a human title or form of respect. I understand that Paul is using the term Lord here (and in other texts such as Romans 9:5 and 10:13) to state Jesus is God (YHVH). This is in part due to the fact that Isaiah 45:23 is quoted in Philippians 2:10 to refer to Jesus and the context of Isaiah clearly applies to YHVH. From my understanding, to acknowledge that Jesus is LORD means He is God, one with the Father (John 10:30). This does not imply that the Father or the Holy Spirit are not God, nor is it to believe in anything that will undermine the clear witness of the Old Testament – of faith in one God (Deuteronomy 6:4), especially as we know the term for 'one' here (in the Hebrew *echad*) indicates composite unity.

I am also convinced that Paul, having encountered the crucified and risen Jesus and knowing the indwelling of the Holy Spirit, could do nothing else but freely join with Thomas and many others and bow down in worship, declaring Jesus – as Lord and King. Here the resurrection is the key for declaring the divinity of Jesus. Indeed the divinity of Jesus is meaningless unless we know in terms of the humanity of Jesus that He had been raised from the dead. Only a resurrected Jesus can be the High Priest constantly interceding for us; only a resurrected Jesus can return to reign and rule, and only a resurrected Jesus can be the firstfruits of the resurrection life promised to His followers.

In regard to the use of the divine Name YHWH, the NIV translation uses the pattern used in most English versions by rendering that name as LORD in capital letters to distinguish it from *Adonai*, another Hebrew word rendered Lord for which lower case letters are used. When the two words stand together in a text as a compound name of God, the term 'Sovereign Lord' is used.

In regard to the use of the divine Name in the MJFB translation, the pattern is to use the word 'Adonai' in capitals followed by 'Elohim' or a derivative of it, whenever used together in a sentence. When the word 'God' appears alone without The Name, the word 'God' is used with the vowel intact as this is viewed as acceptable in both Christian and Jewish Scriptural texts. When God's holy Name is quoted in the New Testament it has already been transliterated into Greek. It is therefore the translators' intention to point the way back to the original (Hebrew) use, so they chose to continue using '*ADONAI*' rather than '*LORD*'. This is done consistently, but only when in the view of the translators the context is specifically calling attention to an Old Testament text. The Greek word *Kurios* is translated 'Lord', for deity; otherwise *Sir or Master* is used. Likewise, since the Spirit of God appears from the earliest verses in Genesis, the translators decided to use *Ruach Elohim*. Unless *Elohim* was part of a conjunction for a title, they simply use 'God'. *Ruach hakodesh* is used consistently for the Holy Spirit.

In addition to the use of the divine Name in the two translations I am using in this study (NIV and MJFB), I would also recommended you look at the translating principles for the *One New Man Bible* (Published by True Potential Publishing), which again adds insight into this important issue. The Glossary section focusing on 'God Incarnate' (pages 1720–1726) is a helpful place to start.

Notes

[1] There is a particular emphasis on the importance of strengthening fellowship, protecting unity, and on knowing and expressing joy in Christian living.

[2] For a study of this text and possible interpretations, see my book *The Case for Enlargement Theology,* Glory to Glory publications, 2010, pages 66–68.

Exploring the third key Christological text

Colossians 1:15–20

He is the image of the invisible God, the firstborn over all creation. For by him all things were created: things in heaven and on earth, visible and invisible, whether thrones or powers or rulers or authorities; all things were created by him and for him. He is before all things, and in him all things hold together. And he is the head of the body, the church; he is the beginning and the firstborn from among the dead, so that in everything he might have the supremacy. For God was pleased to have all his fullness dwell in him, and through him to reconcile to himself all things, whether things on earth or things in heaven, by making peace through his blood, shed on the cross.

Colossians 1:15–20 (NIV)

He is the image of the invisible God, the firstborn of all creation. For by Him all things were created—in heaven and on earth, the seen and the unseen, whether thrones or angelic powers or ruler or authorities. All was created through Him and for Him. He exists before everything, and in Him all holds together. He is the head of the body, His community. He is the beginning, the firstborn from the dead—so that He might come to have first place in all things. For God was pleased to have all His fullness dwell in Him and through Him to reconcile all things to Himself, making peace through the blood of His cross—whether things on earth or things in heaven!

Colossians 1:16–20 (MJFB)

Setting the scene for Colossians

In terms of the four key basic questions, the four introductory 'W's in relation to Colossians 1:15–20, let me try to set the scene by offering the following four 'answers'.

Who wrote the letter? The answer is Paul the apostle. I suggest you turn to the section in the Philippians study to find out background information relating to Paul. The Colossians text clearly states Pauline authorship (1:1 and 4:18), and his authorship was universally accepted in the early Church. The only serious questioning of this view was presented firstly in the nineteenth century by scholars such as Mayerhoff and F C Baur, who argued that the Gnostic heresies which are being addressed in the letter belonged to a significantly later period, namely the early to mid-second century. Also, a few minor literary style issues, such as the high number of subsidiary clauses and the use of many new (to Paul) words, and the letter's close resemblance to the letter to the Ephesians,[1] were all cited to try and gain support for a non-Pauline view. These literary issues are minor, and it does seem clear that Paul's style changed in accordance with the many various themes being addressed and the missionary context at the time of writing. Moreover, the heresies being addressed seem more in line with an incipient and embryonic Gnosticism which would fit in much better (or at least as well) within Paul's ministry time rather than an early or mid-second century date.

With regard to the place and time of writing, my answer is from Rome around AD 60 and probably in the same year as Ephesians and Philemon and just before Philippians. As in the case of the dating of Philippians, some scholars have opted for earlier dates (AD 54–59) and placed the writing as coming from Ephesus or Caesarea.

With regard to the purpose of writing, the first point to make is that (unlike a number of Paul's letters in which he was the founding apostle of the Church he was writing to, or he was writing to Churches of which he had otherwise worked closely), Paul had never visited the Church in Colossae. Paul hears of their faith (1:4) from Epaphras (1:7) who had become a Christian during Paul's three year ministry in Ephesus, and had gone on to share the gospel and help establish the Church in Colossae, after which he visited Paul in Rome.

The second point is that this new Church community was soon facing heretical challenges. While we are not told from the text the precise tenets of these, we can begin to construct some answers based on the positive statements made by Paul to undermine and counteract these heresies and to begin to try and promote true Christian understanding and encourage true Christian living.

As often is the case in Paul's letters, we can only begin to understand the questions he has been asked or the behaviour he is addressing from the answers he gives. So the key purpose in writing this letter is to deal with the heresies which clearly constituted a serious danger to the life of the emerging Church. These heresies clearly were detracting in some way from the centrality of Jesus and undermining His identity. Paul lays great emphasis upon the pre-eminence of Jesus and warns against *hollow and deceptive philosophy, which depends on human tradition and the basic principles of this world rather than on Christ* (2:8). The reference to philosophy and the associated asceticism (2:21–23) points to a Greek influence, yet the reference to tradition and the teaching about circumcision may well point to a Jewish source for the prevailing heresies, or perhaps most likely a fusion of the two.

Turning to the Text

Verses 15–20

These verses are perhaps, as in the case of Philippians 2:6–11,[2] an early Christian hymn (see 3:16) praising the rule of Jesus Christ. There appear to be two segments to these verses, vv. 15-17 (with a focus on creation), and vv. 18–20 (with a focus on the rule of Jesus Christ in redemption and reconciliation).

Paul begins by presenting Jesus as *the image of the invisible God*. This term is also used by Paul in 2 Corinthians 4:4. The meaning of 'image' certainly has connections back to Genesis 1:26–27 and the creation of humanity in the image of God. This image was then to be broken and distorted but not destroyed by Adam's sin resulting in the Fall. Paul certainly uses the contrast of the first Adam with the last Adam (Jesus) in Romans 5 and 1 Corinthians 15:44–49. Yet the meaning of 'image' here for Paul is more than the humanity of Jesus and His incarnation. Indeed, what pertained to Him – His creative powers, His eternal existence, His headship over the universe and the fullness that dwelt in Him (see also 2:6) – belonged to Him before His incarnation. The meaning here is that the being and attributes of God are uniquely and perfectly manifested in the person and work of Jesus. This is also the insight Paul explores in 1 Timothy 3:16.

Jesus is also *the firstborn over all creation*. This cannot mean, from the context of His being the image of God and all which follows in these verses, that Jesus is a created being as opposed to God – this would be highly inconsistent[3] – but rather, Paul is speaking of the privileges held by the firstborn son, the privileges of sovereignty, priority and pre-eminence which are then displayed in the following verses. In some ways the NIV and the MJFB may have been more accurate by using the term *first-begotten* or the phrase *ranking higher* as used in the New Century Version of the New Testament.

He is before all things (v. 17) refers to time, and links to John 1:1 and *in him all things hold together*. Here Paul declares that the moment by moment existence of the whole of the created order, the physical and moral universe, depends on His providential power and care. From this universal creation context Paul shifts the focus on to the relationship between Jesus and the Church and His work in redemption and reconciliation. Here Paul reconnects with the theme introduced in verse 14.

He is the head of the body, the church – here Paul uses the same metaphor as in Ephesians 1:22–23. Moreover, Paul states He is the *firstborn from among the dead*. In this, Paul is declaring that Jesus Christ sustains the highest position over creation and the Church. He is the heir of all things, the exalted Son of God above all. For Paul, the term *fullness* (v. 19) means all the power and attributes of God, while this term 'fullness' (*pleroma* in Greek) was a well-known technical term in Gnostic teaching and means (in this context) the forces which control the fate of people. Maybe Paul is deliberately using this term as part of his engagement with, in order to refute, those promoting heretical (Gnostic) ideas and values.

The goal of the supremacy of Jesus Christ is the reconciliation of all things. Paul develops this theme of reconciliation in 2 Corinthians 5:15–21 and concludes his teaching with the awesome words: *God made him who had no sin be sin for us, so that in him we might become the righteousness of God*.

The reconciling of all things cannot mean that all things are reconciled, for as Paul well knows, many people, including many of his own Jewish brothers (Romans 9:3), are alienated from or opposed to the gospel, yet it points to the ultimate victory of Jesus upon the cross through His sacrificial death, glorious resurrection and the outpouring of His Spirit. The way is now open for all to come to Him: there is no enemy beyond the reach of God's redeeming love; there is no form of alienation which cannot be restored by the Father's welcome. There is no sin which cannot be washed away by Christ's shed blood, and there is no brokenness which cannot now be healed by the indwelling of the Holy Spirit. In all of this the rule and reign of Jesus will be seen, experienced and celebrated.

Notes

[1] It was argued that a later writer used Ephesians as the basic source material for the writing of the letter to the Philippians.

[2] Other examples may well include Ephesians 5:14, John 1:1–4 and 1 Timothy 3:16.

[3] For example, how could a created being be the source of the creation of all things?

Exploring the fourth key Christological text

Hebrews 1:1–4

In the past God spoke to our forefathers through the prophets at many times and in various ways, but in these last days he has spoken to us by his Son, whom he appointed heir of all things, and through whom he made the universe. The Son is the radiance of God's glory and the exact representation of his being, sustaining all things by his powerful word. After he had provided purification for sins, he sat down at the right hand of the Majesty in heaven. So he became as much superior to the angels as the name he has inherited is superior to theirs.

Hebrews 1:1–4 (NIV)

At many times and in many ways, God spoke long ago to the fathers through the prophets. In these last days He has spoken to us through a Son, whom He appointed heir of all things and through whom He created the universe. This Son is the radiance of His glory and the imprint of His being, upholding all things by His powerful word. When He had made purification for our sins, He sat down at the right hand of the Majesty on high. Thus He became as far above the angels as the name He has inherited is more excellent than theirs.

Hebrews 1:1–4 (MJFB)

Setting the Scene

In terms of the four key basic questions, the four introductory 'W's in relation to Hebrews 1:1–4, let me set the scene by offering the following four 'answers'.

Who wrote the letter? The best answer one can give is to refer back to one of the early Church Fathers, Origen of Alexandria, who stated that 'God alone knows'. All we know from the text is that it was written by a man (11:32 – *tell* translates the masculine form of the verb, indicating that the author is male) and almost certainly a Jewish believer in Jesus, well versed in the Torah and the practices and teachings of the Temple priesthood. Traditionally, Paul has been top of the list of suggested authors, followed by Barnabas, Apollos, Clement, Silas and Stephen. Pauline authorship is supported, in part, by the fact that the writer is clearly well known to the first recipients. We see this connection in part by the reference to Timothy (13:23), a close missionary colleague of Paul. Pauline authorship is also supported by the contention of the Church Father Clement of Alexandria (quoted in Eusebius) which states that the letter is Paul's and that it was written first in Hebrew, before being translated into Greek by Luke.

The Greek of this letter is of a more classic style than the common Greek used in the rest of the New Testament writings. Against Pauline authorship is the fact that nowhere in the text does the author identify himself (a usual practice for Paul), and the writing style is markedly different from the other thirteen Pauline letters contained within the New Testament.

I have recently been drawn to the probability of Lukan authorship, and I would suggest readers have a look at the book by David L Allen (see bibliography for details). I particularly found the way in which Allen uses the letter to the Hebrews to help interpret events in Luke's Gospel and the book of Acts to be compelling. Also, in tentative support of building a case for Lukan authorship, there are three other insights or suggestions. Firstly, it is possible that that the Theophilus to whom Luke wrote Luke/Acts (Acts 1:1) is not simply a general title ('beloved of God') but an actual person. This person, Theophilus, was also – it is suggested – a priest, and not only a priest but a high priest. The name Theophilus appears on a list of high priests who served in the period leading up to the destruction of the Temple. If this connection is valid then Luke would have surely had first-hand interest in (and an expert source for insights into) Temple practices and the ministry of the priesthood. Secondly, the writer of Hebrews uses a number of sailing metaphors while offering encouragement. Maybe therefore the writer was familiar with sailing or sea travel. We know Luke went on a number of major sea voyages as part of the missionary journeys he shared with Paul and others.

Finally, the Greek word in Hebrews 4:12 and 11:34 translated in most texts as *two-edged sword* or *sword* can in fact be a specialised term referring to a medical surgical knife rather than a fighting sword. Such a usage would have been known by Doctor Luke. However, against this view it should be noted that the same term is used in John 18:10, and from the context the word is usually translated as *sword*, but the term *dagger* or *knife* could also be viewed as appropriate.

With regard to the place and date of writing, again we cannot be definite. We know from the text that greetings are sent from those in Italy (13:24) which some have taken to mean that it was written to the Church in Rome, but this does not relate directly to the place of writing. Others have suggested the letter was written from (or directed to) Christian communities with a strong Jewish element in places such as Alexandria, Jerusalem or Pella. In terms of date, we know that the writer uses the present tense when describing various Temple practices and sacrifices, which implies the Temple is still fully operational, which would mean a date before AD 70.

The only other clue from the text is that we know that some Jewish believers were being tempted to fall away from the Church and return to the synagogue and the wider non-Messianic Jewish community. Maybe this temptation was fuelled at times by active persecution falling upon the Church and the fact that 'official Judaism' offered a relative level of security within the set-up of the Roman Empire. There were times and places where persecution took root during the early Church period, but we know that there were also times of peace. We know from Paul's letter to the Romans (written around AD 56–57) that the Church in Rome was not facing persecution at the time of his writing, but a few years later, towards the end of Nero's reign, it was.

Therefore the suggestion is that Hebrews is a letter of encouragement addressed to Jewish believers during a time of persecution because, while all believers were targeted in the persecution, only Jewish believers had a clear way out, in that they could return to the synagogue. If this was the case, maybe Hebrews was written to Jewish believers in Rome, who were facing Nero's persecution. Therefore the date of the letter must fall after Jewish people returned to Rome following the suspension of the edict of expulsion issued by Claudius in or around AD 49, and after Paul's letter to the Romans (AD 57–58), and during the extended persecution under the last of the Julio-Claudius dynasty of Emperors, Nero (AD 64–68) and before the destruction of the Temple (AD 70).

As for the purpose in writing, we have already touched on one answer, namely to encourage Jewish believers in Jesus to remain firm in their faith (especially during times of persecution) and this encouragement hopefully would equip them to keep on going forward in their Christian/Messianic Jewish faith and not to deny the Messiah (and reject His once-and-for-all sacrifice upon the cross) and to fall back to the non-Messianic rabbinical communities.

In addition to this, the writer wants to encourage, exhorting and warning the recipients to see and to fully appreciate the greatness of Jesus. The focus on Jesus shows that, whatever the problems and challenges facing the Church, a proper Christology is the key to moving forward. Throughout this letter the Christian life is constantly presented as forward looking: it is a pilgrimage to a goal, to a place of rest (4:11) and a journey to the heavenly city (11:16 and 13:24).

The author of Hebrews could also see that Christology, ecclesiology and mission are intimately connected. Jesus is *better* than that which has gone before – better not just in terms of degree, but in terms of essence. There is an 'intrinsic superiority' about the person and work of Jesus. Throughout the letter to the Hebrews there is a clear direction of travel from lesser to greater. This reminds me of the Jewish idiom in the Gospels, when Jesus speaks in terms of *how much more* (in Matthew 7:11 and Luke 11:13), and also in Paul's teaching (for example Romans 11:12 and 11:24). God's loving purposes are being 'enlarged' through Jesus. Jesus brings a 'better covenant' (7:22) and 'better sacrifices' (9:23) and a 'better word' (12:24), therefore don't turn back, keep belonging to Jesus, keep loving each other as brothers (13:1), keep doing good and sharing with others (13:16), and keep on following and proclaiming to all people the good news of Jesus, who is the true pioneer and the perfect high priest.

This dual understanding of Jesus as pioneer and priest also helps shape the Christology presented in this letter. Furthermore, the Christology of Hebrews is shaped by numerous references or allusions to Psalm 110 (quoted more frequently in the New Testament[1] than any other Old Testament passage). In the time of Jesus, this psalm was understood to be one that focused on the Messiah and especially His exaltation. Within the Psalm there is also reference (v. 4) to the priestly order of Melchizedek, a theme which makes up a large section of the teaching in Hebrews (chapters 7–8). In many ways a strong argument can be made[2] for seeing Psalm 110 as the key source for the development of many aspects of Christology in the early Church.

Finally, it is important to say that the assertion and celebration of the supremacy of Jesus Christ over and above the Jewish Temple practices should not be understood as a polemical anti-Semitic attack on Jewish institutions, but better understood as part of an internal Jewish dispute, and as a way of demonstrating the greatness of Jesus Christ and the significance of the gospel, especially for a Jewish religious audience. The significance of the gospel to a Jewish audience is given theological and practical momentum in the teaching of Paul (see, for example, Romans 1:16, and Romans 9–11).

Turning to the text

Verses 1–4

In the Greek text these four verses are one single sentence of 72 words. These words make up an awesome prologue to the letter. The epistle is primarily a pastoral letter to Jewish believers in Jesus, but it also gives to the Church a key evangelistic resource, especially for reaching out to many Jewish people.

This opening sentence takes the reader on a huge journey, from the very act of creation (v. 2) to the consummation of all things (v. 3). This 'alpha to omega' journey is focussed in and through Jesus, who is identified in this text as the Son. The identification of Him as Son rather than the Word (as in John1:1) or the image of the invisible God (as in Colossians 1:15) or some other description, is to emphasise relationship. A son must have a Father; a father must have an offspring.

Both the terms 'Father' and 'Son' are mutually defined by an inherent relationship.

In terms of the characteristics of God, in addition to the Father/Son relationship the text declares two other key points. Firstly, God is a God who speaks – He is committed to revelation, to making things known. In the past, revelation has occurred through four main ways: in the giving of the Scriptures; through the act of creation itself (see, for example, Romans 1:20/Psalm 8); through the outworking of history (the Bible makes clear that history is linear and is moving towards a goal), and through our own God-shaped consciousness, which is part of what it means to be made 'in the image of God'. Yet these valuable revelatory gifts are not sufficient in themselves, for without the decisive and timely revelatory act through the Son we would remain helpless and hopeless.

Secondly, God is faithful to His past revelation. For example, the letter to the Hebrews quotes directly from all three areas of previously revealed scripture: the Torah, the Prophets and the Writings. This revelation is authoritative, yet there is a sense in which it is partial and contextually limited; there is need for more. The contrast is clearly stated between the past (to our forefathers) and through the prophets to the present (in these days), to us through the Son. The emphasis on the Son, as stated earlier, affirms relationship within the nature of God, while also it connects with the wider New Testament revelation that the gospel is "Son-shaped" (see for example John 3:16 and Romans 1:9). This opening part of the letter makes it clear that the Son brings a personal, complete and final revelation.

In addition to these points, the writer then declares seven[3] things about the Son. Perhaps this reference to seven connects to the Hebrew notion of seven as a pointer to a sense of wholeness and completion, or perhaps it refers to the seven things (including the pre-existent name of the Messiah) which the Talmud states were created before the world was created, or even maybe the focus of seven is a rhetorical device pointing to a comparison between knowing Jesus and knowing the seven wonders of the ancient world.[4]

These seven wonders relating to Jesus are as follows:

The Son is the appointed heir of all things.

The Father gives the Son all authority.

The Son is the agent of creation.

The Son is the radiance of God's glory.

The key point here is just as the brilliance of the sun in the midday sky is inseparable from the sun itself, so the Son's radiance is inseparable from our speaking of and our experiencing of God. However the Greek here points to even more – namely, Jesus is Himself the source of this radiance, giving out, not simply reflecting. For as the Father is, so is the Son. Here the awesome dignity, beauty and exalted rank of the Son of God are declared.

The Son is the exact representation of His being.

The key point here is that just as a seal is made by a perfect impression, so Jesus is the exact impression and bears the authentic stamp and the perfect image of God. The Greek word *character* only appears here in the New Testament and is translated in the NIV as *exact representation,* and in the MJFB as *imprint of His glory.* The writer in using this unique (in regard to New Testament usage) word conveys an even stronger and clearer message than the message conveyed simply by the use of the word *eikon*, translated as 'image' in 2 Corinthians 4:4 and Colossians 1:15. The writer is wanting to build upon the word *apaugasma* used earlier in the sentence, translated as 'radiance', to declare that the very essence of God is fully manifested in Jesus and this manifestation is unique and permanent. In this sense I believe the writer is wanting to explain the nature of Jesus the Son, both as He reveals the Father and as he relates to the Father.

Here we are talking about more than a perfect image, as in a perfect waxwork portrayal of a person, but rather, Jesus is the very expression of God and is being of the 'same substance'. The term 'of the same substance' became very important in later credal statements. In using the term 'same substance' one is simply anglicising the Latin word *substantia* from the Greek, meaning in this context 'essence' rather than simply 'matter'. In popular language we could say that Jesus is 'made of the exact same stuff' as God, which may be helpful, but there is always a danger in trying to popularise or update carefully crafted theological words which have endured much scrutiny, from both friend and foe.

The Son sustains all things by his powerful word.

The key point here is that the Son holds the whole universe together – from the microscopic level to the infinite expanses of expanding space. In terms of the pastoral and evangelistic application of this truth, I would want to try and say: if He holds all this together, He can surely hold your life together, even at times it appears to be broken or spinning out of control. What you must do is yield your life to Him as your Saviour and Lord.

The Son makes purification for sin.

He did this through His redeeming death on the cross (see, for example, 2 Corinthians 5:21). The truth which shocks and challenges here is that, despite all that the writer declares about the infinite greatness of the Son, the Son died upon a cross. Here He makes purification – not by speaking a word as in the act of creation, but by His action, His becoming the atoning sacrifice. In this act Jesus is separated from the Father in a way unknown throughout eternity. In terms of our understanding of eternity it should be noted that eternity contains (holds) time. The act of the atoning sacrifice of Jesus is rooted in time (and in a specific historical event in a specific place) and yet it is beyond time and place. This is why the book of Revelation (13:8) for example can declare that the Lamb (Jesus) was *slain from the creation of the world*.

He sat down at the right hand of the Majesty in heaven. In this phrase there is an allusion to Psalm 110:1 (as stated earlier). Psalm 110 is a predominant refrain throughout the letter to the Hebrews. Here the focus is on completion and honour. The High Priest never sat down in the Holy of Holies, yet Jesus completed His work and calling as prophet, priest and King.

Let us be encouraged as we walk along the ancient path of Christological study, and as we enjoy the views may we celebrate the person and work of Jesus. For in Jesus the true vision of God is perfectly expressed, the revelation of God is *displayed in the face* of Christ (see 2 Corinthians 4:6), and in seeing Jesus, one has seen the Father.

Notes

[1] There are 33 direct quotations spanning Matthew, Mark, Luke, Acts, 1 Corinthians, Ephesians, Colossians, 1 Peter and Hebrews.

[2] To understand this argument and for a wider reflection on Psalm 110, see the Olive Press Research Paper *Risen and Exalted,* by Frank Booth, (Issue 21, 2014). This paper can be downloaded free from the CMJ UK website.

[3] See also the use of patterns of seven in the structuring of John's Gospel as noted in the section on turning to the text in exploring John 1:1-18.

[4] It may be that the writer is saying something along the lines that these seven man-made wonders – the great pyramid at Giza, the hanging gardens at Babylon, the Statue of Zeus at Olympia, the Temple of Archemis at Ephesus, the mausoleum at Bodrum, the Statue to Helios (Greek god of the sun) in Rhodes and the lighthouse of Alexandria – are all nothing compared to seeing the glory of Jesus. Paul uses a similar rhetoric style when declaring the supremacy of knowing Jesus in Philippians 3:8.

Exploring Christian Mission and our Understanding of God

(a) Taking the first steps – back to the beginning

The first steps along the ancient path of Christological study begin in the very beginning. We were reminded of this in our study of John 1, the first of our four Christological texts. *In the beginning* places our first Christological steps in the great monotheistic revelation of God in the Old Testament. Here we gain understanding about God's character, name, purposes, attributes and covenantal faithfulness.

At the heart of this revelation is the *Shema* (Deuteronomy 6:4) which defines Jewish faith identity and declares the existence, identity, unity and power of God: *Hear O Israel, The Lord our God, the Lord is one*. Yet in understanding Christology in terms of the divinity of Jesus and the wider Trinitarian doctrines, it is important to note that the *Shema* does not undermine Christology or a Trinitarian doctrine of God. I understand that the mystery of Christology and the Trinity is in fact spurred on by the unwavering witness to the One God in the Old Testament scriptures. Yet the full truth is only fully revealed in the witness of the New Testament.

This revelation was then codified into a consensus of Christian orthodox thought by the fourth century. It is beyond the scope of this brief book to outline the hard fought for nature of gaining such a consensus, but the consensus was based on two core truths of Trinitarian understanding: firstly, the clear distinction between the three interrelated, and equal 'persons' of the Godhead; and secondly, the unequivocal affirmation of the one divine essence of the One God, the Holy Trinity.

The term for 'one' in the Shema (*echad* in Hebrew) does

not refer to simple singularity, but allows for at the very least a sense of unity in plurality, while a strong case can be made for saying the term definitely implies composite unity. It is used when speaking about a husband and wife becoming one flesh or a group of people being of one mind and pursuing one path of action. The later rabbinical Jewish ruling out of 'unity in plurality' has nothing to do with the revelation of Scripture but rests upon the thirteen articles of rabbinical Jewish faith espoused by Maimonides (AD 1135–1204) and formulated in his commentary on the Mishnah. Some of his insights were drawn from Aristotelian and rationalistic philosophy, rather than from Scriptural revelation. It is important to state that aspects of the Trinitarian understanding of one God are not such an alien concept to those holding a Jewish Biblical worldview, as so very many contemporary rabbis would try to insist, but rather a Trinitarian view is alien to this later reformulated rabbinical worldview, as reflected in the writing and thinking of Maimonides.

It is also important to understand and explore in regard to this reformulated rabbinical worldview, that there is not an unbroken line of theological development from the Old Testament (as many rabbis would claim) to rabbinical teaching today, but there are many elements of 'discontinuity'. For example, following the destruction of the Temple, rabbinical Judaism removed a core aspect of its religious life, namely the focus on substitutionary sacrifice as a key requirement in dealing with sin and approaching God.

(b) Talking along the way
– Joining in with a missional conversation

In addition to this re-appraisal of the Shema, there is much else within the Old Testament which gives a foundation for the divinity of the Messiah and a wider Trinitarian understanding of God.

In initial discussions with Jewish friends, and to a lesser extent within Islamic contexts, it has become clearer to me that both rabbinical Judaism and Islam are locked into a monotheistic concept which denies the Son. In Islamic thought God has no Son. This core belief is inscribed on the Dome of the Rock in Jerusalem, where part of the inscription reads: 'God is only one God and far be it from his glory that he should have a son.' Maybe this Islamic denial of the Son has its roots in some way in the hurt relating to Ishmael's own rejection by Abraham.

Similarly, rabbinical Jewish theology also teaches that God has no Son and proclaims that 'God will not share His glory with another.' It is this denial of the Son which causes the fundamental alienation from God and from one another. As stated in the introduction, our view of who Jesus is and what He does is indeed the key demarcation point in all our missional endeavours. My understanding is that these half-brothers, the sons of Ishmael and the sons of Isaac, will only be restored to God's family and His perfect purposes when both freely and joyfully acknowledge the true Son. As Christians and Messianic Jews, we are united in proclaiming the gospel of His Son (Romans 1:9). This gospel message provides the only hope for our dysfunctional world. In further reflection on sharing the gospel and establishing authentic missional conversations, primarily in a Jewish context, I have found it helpful to focus on the following three areas.

Firstly, it helps if we consider the use of the divine Name, based on a study beginning in Exodus 3 with Moses, the burning bush and the ineffable Name of God. The Name of God is both the single most striking and characteristic literary feature of Scripture and the unique linguistic token that signifies the essence and uniqueness of God. This Name is indeed a personal name, without a descriptive content. Our understanding of one God, Father, Son and Holy Spirit, however provides vital content. The titles 'Father', 'Son' and 'Holy Spirit' provide a wonderful summary of the gospel. In regard to the gospel, there are two core truths which we need to know about Jesus: His divine identity and His identity with us! In the unfolding of the gospel we see the Father sends the Son to comfort (Isaiah 40:1) and to save, both in a physical sense (Mathew 14:29–33) and in a fuller and eternal spiritual sense. Jesus carries out the Father's purposes and does so in the power of the Holy Spirit – and, in the power of the Holy Spirit, gives self-designation as Lord. This is seen for example in Mark 11:3. The use of 'Lord' here is the surrogate for the divine name that the crowds shortly used when declaring the truth of Psalm 118:25–26, *Blessed is he who comes in the name of the Lord*. Equally, no one can have faith in Jesus as Lord without the help of the Holy Spirit (1 Corinthians 12:3).

Jesus is quite literally the one who comes in the Name, throughout the New Testament, and especially in the four Christological texts, but also throughout John's Gospel (see the seven I AM sayings) and by the concluding verse of Matthew (28:16), as well as in many other of the New Testament letters and the book of Revelation. The revelation of the New Testament declares that the divine essence is common (equal and undivided) in the 'relational oneness' of the Father, Son and Holy Spirit, In one sense the Father gives the divine Name, the Son receives it and the Holy Spirit glorifies it and brings it into a universal mission context by equipping the Church with the gifts of ministry and service.

In this context the concept of 'divinity' is best understood as the total sum of the attributes of God. These attributes express linguistically, doctrinally and foundationally the truth about who God is, in line with His self-revelation, help us to understand His uniqueness, and demarcate biblical boundaries to the way in which we are to think and speak of Him.

Divinity is therefore indivisible and cannot be taken,

imparted or earned. Divinity has no beginning and no end. There are some attributes which can be shared in a relative sense with others, hence humanity bears the image of God, while others are imparted through the new birth in Christ and the indwelling of the Holy Spirit, yet some attributes are attributes which cannot be shared: these 'incommunicable attributes' belong to God alone.

Secondly, I think there is much value in studying the many appearances of the Angel of the Lord who is, I believe, a manifestation of the pre-incarnate Son of God (there may be some distorted echoes of the Biblical witness to the Angel of the Lord picked up in the Talmudic references to Metatron and also to the Trinitarian understanding of God within the later Kabbalistic 'linking' of God, Torah and Israel). These appearances are often referred to as theophanies, from the Greek meaning the 'showing or seeing of God'. These appearances also link back to the eternal Word of God (*Memra* in Aramaic) and the 'Spirit of God' as referenced in Genesis chapter 1, especially in reference to the creation of humankind in God's own image.

The first Biblical theophany is in relation to Hagar in Genesis 16. This is then followed by further theophanies in Genesis 22, 31, 32; Exodus 3, 13, 14; Judges 13, Isaiah 63, etc. It is worth noting in reflecting on these appearances, four initial things. (1) People see the Angel of the Lord yet they do not die as a result of this encounter, as Exodus 33:20 states would happen. This is because death follows the direct appearance of God the Father (the first 'person' of the Trinity) whereas here the pre-incarnate Jesus appears, so the appearance does not lead to immediate death, but to new revelation. The fullness of this revelation is to be seen in John 14:9, *Anyone who has seen me has seen the Father.* (2) In Exodus 3, the Angel of the Lord uses the divine Name. (3) In Isaiah 63, it is stated that God will be the saviour of His people, yet it is the Angel of His presence that is the agent of this, the saving work (Isaiah 63:9). It is also of interest to note in this Isaiah passage the references to the Holy Spirit, both in regard to grieving the Holy Spirit and to experiencing the Holy Spirit – both concepts that feature strongly in the pastoral teaching of the New Testament. As we know Jesus is the only Saviour, it seems right to confidently assert that the Angel of the Lord's presence here in Isaiah is the pre-incarnate Jesus. (4) While angels play a big part in the Gospels, nowhere is there mention of the 'Angel of the Lord', and this is because, following the incarnation, Jesus could not appear in two places at the same time.

Thirdly, I think it is essential to keep focused on who Jesus is and what He does. While in some Jewish circles there is a reluctance to engage in systematic Biblical Theology (and certainly and understandably a reluctance to engage with Church theological history and Trinitarian developments), an engagement with the Jewish Jesus of the Gospels is much more likely to be compelling. Here we can explore the Messianic prophecies which are fulfilled in Jesus; here we can unpack the beauty and power of His Torah faithful life, His ministry in the power of the Holy Spirit, His teaching focused on the Kingdom and discipleship (both concepts firmly rooted in the Judaism – or perhaps more accurately the Judaisms – of the Second Temple period), His mighty acts of deliverance, healing and forgiveness, and His selfless death and glorious resurrection. This focus on Jesus is vital as we rarely see the truth though theological arguments alone but through personal encounters, just as one seldom appreciates the power of music by noting chord structures or debating tonal frequencies, but by hearing, dancing and playing.

(c) Thinking more thoughts – a little more theology for the walk ahead

Based on this rich Scriptural background and on these four key New Testament readings, I understand, as I walk along the ancient Christological path, that Jesus of Nazareth is the living-out in fullness of the divine eternal Word in humanity and is in perfect relationship with the Father through the Holy Spirit. The acts of Jesus are indeed the acts of God, and from this understanding flows a renewal of the doctrine of the Trinity. This is because faith in Jesus is faith in God. Such saving faith is only possible by the power of the Spirit of God at work in us. All Christian theology must be Trinitarian, as the very acts of revelation and atonement are rooted in God, the Father, the Son (the incarnate Word) and the Holy Spirit. The God who speaks comes to save us in the Son and to renew us in the Spirit.

I also understand that Jesus is fully 'anointed' in humanity and in divinity. This is at the very heart of Christology. There is no 'gap' between the divine and the human in Jesus. We cannot speak helpfully about the two halves of Jesus, but rather Jesus is the fully divine presence fully translated into the human individuality of the divine Word. Or, to express this truth in another way: in Jesus, human nature is complete in every aspect as is the divine nature complete in every aspect. This is the identifying unity of the Word becoming flesh. The divine and the human come together in unity (not in competition) in the one person of Jesus.

In reflecting on this, I see Jesus as the most compelling, most complete, most real, most beautiful and most truly human person ever, yet I am also reminded of the prayerful and faith-inspired words of the Christian mystic Julian of Norwich (1342–1413): 'Wherever Jesus appears, the Trinity is understood!'

The whole enterprise of Christology (and Trinitarian

reflection) encounters the problem and restrictions of language. In Christian study maybe it is good that language begins to fail us at some point, because the awesome truth of God must stretch our language and our understanding beyond our limits. We are aware that God is the transcendent Creator of all, and consequently cannot be fully contained by human language or human concepts. For myself, I sense this 'limitation' in speaking of the 'persons' of God within Trinitarian discussions. God is indeed personal, yet not in the same way that created beings are persons. This is why theology is about faith seeking understanding, and not about intellectual convictions seeking systematic expressions of understanding.

Maybe at the heart of Christology is the understanding that we can only speak about God meaningfully in terms of relationships. We think of the relationships within the Godhead – Father, Son and Holy Spirit, which are His very essence. We think too of our own relationship with God, our relationships with each other within the community of faith and our experience of being human – body, mind and spirit.

Paul teaches in many ways about who Jesus is (He is the agent of divine judgement, the giver of the Holy Spirit/ the Lord/ the mediator/ the new Adam, etc.), yet when Paul teaches in this way, he takes our understanding of Jesus beyond 'only the human'.

Paul also rejects the various theological constructs, available to him, such as Tritheism (which teaches belief in three gods), or Unitarianism (which upholds the 'oneness of God', yet clearly denies any belief in the divinity of Jesus and of the Holy Spirit), or Modalism (which teaches that God appears at different times in different 'persons', sometimes as the Father, or as the Son, or as the Holy Spirit) or Adoptionism (which teaches that the human Jesus became God at a specific point during His ministry – most probably at His baptism) or some form of syncretistic polytheism (which presents a view of many gods and spirits merging to inhabit and to be absorbed into the cosmos).

As stated, all of these theological constructs (and their numerous variations) were freely available in the rich eschatological and theological mix provided by late Second Temple Judaism(s) and its engagement with the wider pagan world. Yet Paul (like all of the New Testament writers) again rejects all these available theological options, and he and others push forward into new territory based on new revelation. There is a clear rejection of easier and perhaps more ostensibly logical and well-trodden paths by stressing, again and again, the real human suffering and humanity of Jesus, alongside His essential divine character and Spirit-empowered actions. There is a richness of revelation as the Apostle communicates a contemporary and a faithful 'yes' to all he has experienced in encountering the risen Lord and in yielding to His Spirit, while remaining faithful to all the revelation of the past which prevents him from violating Biblical monotheism and entering into idolatry.

Paul's Christology teaches that we cannot have an unmediated relationship with God the Father: the mediator is Jesus. God in Christ rescues us not by displacing anything human but by restoring by grace. This enables us to enjoy being in Christ and being adopted as children of God. Let me give to Paul the final word, by quoting from a text which is sometimes spoken of as the New Testament Shema, (1 Corinthians 8:6):

... yet for us there is but one God, the Father, from whom all things came and for whom we live; and there is but one Lord, Jesus Christ, through whom all things came, and through whom we live.

NIV

... yet for us there is one God, the Father, from whom are all things, and we exist for Him; and one Lord, Yeshua the Messiah, through whom are all things, and we exist through Him.

MJFB

SOME RESOURCES FOR REFLECTION

My working definition of the Trinity

The faith based understanding that there is only one God, but in the unity of the Godhead there are three eternal and co-equal Persons: the Father, the Son and the Holy Spirit, the same in substance or essence, but distinct in subsistence or existence.

Definition of the Trinity based on the teaching of Louis Berkhof

There is in the Divine Being but one indivisible essence. God is one in His essential being (constitutional nature). In the one Divine Being there are three persons or individual subsistences, Father, Son and Holy Spirit. The whole undivided essence of God belongs equally to each of the three persons. The subsistence and operation of the three persons in the Divine Being is marked by a definite order and by certain attributes by which the persons are distinguished. This Trinity is a confession of the Church and is a mystery beyond the full comprehension of man.

Definition of the Trinity from the Encyclopaedia of the Reformed Faith

The one and only God is the threefold reality of Father, Son and Holy Spirit.

The Nicene Creed (AD 325)

We believe in one God, the Father, the Almighty, maker of heaven and earth, of all that is, seen and unseen.

We believe in one Lord, Jesus Christ, the only Son of God, eternally begotten of the Father, God from God, Light from Light, true God from true God, begotten, not made, of one Being with the Father. Through him all things were made. For us and for our salvation he came down from heaven: by the power of the Holy Spirit he became incarnate from the Virgin Mary, and was made man. For our sake he was crucified under Pontius Pilate; he suffered death and was buried. On the third day he rose again in accordance with the Scriptures; he ascended into heaven and is seated at the right hand of the Father. He will come again in glory to judge the living and the dead, and his kingdom will have no end.

We believe in the Holy Spirit, the Lord, the giver of life, who proceeds from the Father [and the Son]. With the Father and the Son he is worshipped and glorified. He has spoken through the Prophets. We believe in one holy catholic and apostolic Church. We acknowledge one baptism for the forgiveness of sins. We look for the resurrection of the dead, and the life of the world to come. Amen.

The Westminster Confession of Faith (AD 1646)
Parts 1 and 3 of the statement of God, and the Holy Trinity

There is but one only living and true God, who is infinite in being and perfection, a most pure spirit, invisible, without body, parts, or passions, immutable, immense, eternal, incomprehensible, almighty, most wise, most holy, most free, most absolute, working all things according to the counsel of his own immutable and most righteous will, for his own glory, most loving, gracious, merciful, long-suffering, abundant in goodness and truth, forgiving iniquity, transgression, and sin; the rewarder of them that diligently seek him; and withal most just and terrible in his judgments; hating all sin; and who will by no means clear the guilty.

In the unity of the Godhead there be three persons of one substance, power, and eternity: God the Father, God the Son, and God the Holy Ghost. The Father is of none, neither begotten nor proceeding; the Son is eternally begotten of the Father; the Holy Ghost eternally proceeding from the Father and the Son.

A Collect for Advent Sunday

Almighty God, you have given your only begotten Son to take our nature upon him, and to be born of a pure virgin. Grant that we, who have been born again and made your children by adoption and grace, may daily be renewed by your Holy Spirit through our Lord Jesus Christ, to whom with you and the same Spirit be honour and glory, now and for ever. Amen.

A Collect for Trinity Sunday

Almighty and eternal God, You have revealed yourself as Father, Son and Holy Spirit. Enable us to live by the Spirit, that, walking with Christ and rejoicing in Your fatherly love, we may become partakers of the mystery of Your divine being: through Jesus Christ our Lord, who lives and reigns with the Father in the unity of the Holy Spirit, three persons in one indivisible God, for ever and ever. Amen

A quote from St Bernard of Clairvaux

How can plurality consist with unity, or unity with plurality? To examine the fact closely is rashness, to believe it is true piety, to know it is life, and life eternal.

A quote from Thomas a Kempis

All is glory and beauty come from within, and there He delights to dwell. His visits there are frequent, His conversation sweet, His comforts refreshing, His peace passing all understanding.

In addition to these historical quotes and credal statements it is also good to hear a number of modern worship songs which present a clear Christology. The following four songs are a helpful place to start:

Let your Glory fall (David Ruis) Vineyard Publishing 1992.

How great is our God (Chris Tomlin, Jesse Reeves and Ed Cash) Sixsteps Music 2004.

At your Name (Tim Hughes and Phil Wickham) Thankyou music 2011.

O This God (Matt Redman and Jonas Myrin) Thankyou Music 2011.

BIBLIOGRAPHY

John's Gospel Study

Fenton J C, *The Gospel according to John,* Oxford University Press, 1970.

Marsh John, *Saint John,* Pelican, 1968.

Neyrey Jerome H, *The Gospel of John,* Cambridge University Press, 2007.

Porter Stanley E, *John, His Gospel and Jesus,* Eerdmans, 2015.

Richardson Alan, *The Gospel according to Saint John,* SCM, 1959.

Philippians Study

Fee Gordon D, *Paul's Letter to the Philippians,* Eerdmans, 1995.

Grayston Kenneth, *The Letters of Paul to the Philippians and to the Thessalonians,* Cambridge University Press,1967.

Hawthorne Gerald F, *Philippians* (Word Biblical Commentary), Word Books, 1983.

Martin Ralph P, *Philippians,* Oliphants, 1976.

Colossians Study

Dunn James D G, *The Epistle to the Colossians and to Philemon,* Eerdmans, 1996.

Moo Douglas J, *The Letters to the Colossians and to Philemon,* PNTC, 2008.

O'Brien Peter T, *Colossians and Philemon* (Word Biblical Commentary), Word Books, 1982.

Yates Roy, *The Epistle to the Colossians,* Epworth, 1993.

Hebrews Study

Allen David, *Lukan Authorship of Hebrews,* Broadman and Holman, 2010.

Bruce F F, *The Epistle to the Hebrews,* Eerdmans, 1964.

Gordon Robert P, *Hebrews,* Sheffield Academic Press, 2000.

Johnson Luke Timothy, *Hebrews – A Commentary,* Westminster/John Knox Press, 2006.

Lincoln Andrew, *Hebrews – A Guide,* T and T Clark, 2006.

McKelvey R J, *Pioneer and Priest – Jesus Christ in the Epistle to the Hebrews,* Pickwick, 2013.

Riggans Walter, *Hebrews,* Christian Focus Publications, 1998.

Christological and Missional Study

Bauckam Richard, *Jesus and the God of Israel,* Paternoster, 2008.

Berkhof Louis, *Systematic Theology,* Banner of Truth, 1939.

Frey Joseph, *Joseph and Benjamin, A series of letters on the controversy between Jews and Christians*. First published by Daniel Franshaw, in 1840, and republished as *The Divinity of the Messiah,* by Keren Ahva Meshichit, 2012.

Gunton Colin E, *The One, The Three and The Many,* Cambridge University Press 1993.

Harvey Richard, Mapping *Messianic Jewish Theology,* Paternoster, 2009.

Jacob Alex, *The Case for Enlargement Theology,* Glory to Glory, 2010.

—*Prepare the Way!* , Glory to Glory, 2014.

Jocz Jakob, *The Jewish People and Jesus Christ,* SPCK, 1949.

Kirk Kenneth E, *The Vision of God – The Christian Doctrine of the Summum Bonum,* James Clarke Press, 1931.

Marshall Bruce, *Trinity and Truth,* Cambridge University Press, 2000.

Morris Paul, *Jewish Themes in the New Testament,* Paternoster, 2013.

Natan Yoel, *The Jewish Trinity,* Aventine Press, 2003.
Nessim Daniel and Surrey Mark, *Introducing Your Jewish Friends to Yeshua,* Chosen People Ministries, 2010.
Skarsaune Oskar, *In the Shadow of the Temple – Jewish Influences on Early Christianity,* IVP, 2002.
Soulen R Kendall, *The Divine Name(s) and the Holy Trinity,* Westminster/John Knox Press, 2011.
Stirling Andrew (Editor), *The Trinity – An Essential for Faith in Our Time,* Evangel Publishing House, 2002.

Also by Alex Jacob

RECEIVE THE TRUTH!
A collection of
Twenty Questions and Ten Bible Talks
focusing on key issues in contemporary
Christian-Jewish relations
and Christian spirituality

and

PREPARE THE WAY!

How does the birth and subsequent ministry of Jesus connect with the big picture of God's past promises and future purposes? Alex Jacob explores the wider theme through the Church's traditional preparation for Christmas during its 'advent' season – when it focuses upon four key 'players' in the build-up to Christ's birth: the Patriarchs, the Prophets, John the Baptist, and Mary the mother of Jesus. Do not be fooled! This is not just a Christmas book! The themes explored cover 2000 years of God's dealings with people up to the birth of Jesus in Bethlehem, and look forward to His return in glory. Written in an accessible yet authoritative style, this is a helpful resource, suitable for private and group study. It sheds fresh light on God's faithfulness and on issues of our own personal discipleship.

Also by Alex Jacob

THE CASE FOR ENLARGEMENT THEOLOGY

• What are the failings of Replacement Theology?

• What caused the schism between early Christianity and Rabbinical Judaism?

• What theological tools do we need to engage in Jewish-Christian relations?

• How should we interpret the terms 'Israel', 'the church' and 'God's people'?

• How should we understand and apply Paul's teaching in Romans 9-11?

• How should we evaluate the contemporary emergence of the Jewish Messianic movement?

• How should the "Jewish roots" of Christianity translate into contemporary theological models?

• How and why should Christians share the gospel with Jewish people?

This book develops and explores the theme of Enlargement Theology and provides answers to these and many other key questions in the field of Jewish-Christian relations and Biblical Studies. In this exciting study a new theological model is presented which breaks down the barriers resulting from both Replacement Theology (Supersessionism) and Two Covenant Theology.

For all who are seeking to engage in a biblically faithful and astute way within the field of Jewish-Christian relations.

available from:
www.cmj.org.uk